The Wild Outdoors

T0045308

 **BOWHUNTING!**

by
Lisa M. Bolt Simons

CAPSTONE PRESS
a capstone imprint

Captivate is published by Capstone Press, an imprint of Capstone.
1710 Roe Crest Drive, North Mankato, Minnesota 56003
www.capstonepub.com

Library of Congress Cataloging-in-Publication Data
Names: Simons, Lisa M. B., 1969- author.
Title: Go bowhunting! / by Lisa M. Bolt Simons.
Description: North Mankato, Minnesota : Capstone Press, [2022] |
Series: The wild outdoors | Includes bibliographical references and index.
| Audience: Ages 8-11 | Audience: Grades 4-6 | Summary: "Whether it's a
rabbit, a deer, or something even bigger, nothing is more exciting than the
thrill of the hunt. This is especially true when your weapon requires the
skill and precision of a bow and arrow. Readers will learn about the gear
bow hunters use and get step-by-step instructions on how to safely shoot a
bow and arrow"— Provided by publisher.
Identifiers: LCCN 2021002817 (print) | LCCN 2021002818 (ebook) |
ISBN 9781663905994 (hardcover) | ISBN 9781663920454 (paperback) |
ISBN 9781663905963 (pdf) | ISBN 9781663905987 (kindle edition)
Subjects: LCSH: Bowhunting—Juvenile literature.
Classification: LCC SK36 .S56 2022 (print) | LCC SK36 (ebook) |
DDC 799.2/15—dc23
LC record available at https://lccn.loc.gov/2021002817
LC ebook record available at https://lccn.loc.gov/2021002818

Image Credits
Alamy: Friedrich Saurer, 23, parm, 29; Getty Images: CHRISTOPHE
SIMON/Staff, 21, Mitch Kezar/Design Pics, 9; Newscom: Mitch Kezar,
18; Shutterstock: 9387388673, Cover, Andrei Tony, 11, (left), Andrey
Burmakin, 13, (right), Belish, 15, Bruce MacQueen, 5, Keith Publicover,
11, (right), maradon 333, 7, Menno Schaefer, 27, Nate Allred, 16, Nicholas
Rjabow, 12, Olga Popova, 13, (left), Paul Tessier, 22, Paul Tessier, 28,
Sarbinaz, 14, Stefan Malloch, 24, Stock image, 1, StudioByTheSea, 17

Editorial Credits
Editor: Mandy Robbins; Designer: Jennifer Bergstrom; Media Researcher:
Morgan Walters; Production Specialist: Tori Abraham

This book is dedicated to the memory of Aidan D. Miller,
an avid outdoorsman who was loved by many.

Table of Contents

Words in **bold** are in the glossary.

ON THE HUNT!

It's quiet in the woods. You stay as still as possible. You can't move. You can't make a sound. You don't want to scare away the prize you've come to hunt.

You're up in a tree stand, dressed in **camouflage** from head to toe. Your bow and arrow are ready. You wait for a deer to come closer.

Your blood pumps as a huge buck walks out from behind a bush. He heads into your line of sight. Your heart starts to race. The deer has to be close for your shot to be **precise**. Your aim has to be almost perfect. He walks closer, not sensing you. You slowly raise your bow and take the shot!

Chapter 1

AN ANCIENT TRADITION

Shooting with a bow and arrow is called **archery**. Experts believe that people in Africa made bows and arrows more than 60,000 years ago. The practice eventually spread. There is evidence that archery was used in Egypt as far back as 3,000 BCE and in China by the 1700s BCE. People used bows and arrows for both hunting and battle in times of war.

Ancient bows and arrows have been found on five continents. In North America, American Indians relied on bowhunting in their daily lives. They used every part of the bison and elk they hunted—for food, clothing, and shelter—everything the people needed.

Ancient rock carvings from 5,000 years ago show people bowhunting.

The traditional bow and arrow used throughout history was called the longbow. It was built with a long, straight limb that curved back when strung.

Throughout history, bowhunters worked hard to become skilled and experienced archers. That's still true today. It takes time and practice to shoot well with a bow and arrow.

So why would someone bowhunt today when shotguns and rifles are so much easier? There are many reasons. Bowhunting is more challenging. The hunter has to be a lot quieter than when hunting with a gun. That's because hunters must be closer to the animals they are hunting. If they're too far away, they may miss the shot. This makes the hunt more exciting.

Some hunters like using bows and arrows because they are quieter than guns. Other hunters feel bows and arrows are safer than using other weapons. Some simply enjoy using bows and arrows more than using guns.

A bowhunter aims an arrow carefully.

Chapter 2

GEARED UP TO GO

If you want to bowhunt, you need the right gear. There are two main types of bows used for hunting. The recurve bow is a traditional bow. It has been used since bows were invented. The compound bow is a fairly new invention. This bow has pulleys for the string. You don't need as much strength to **draw** back the arrow in the bow.

When you get a bow, you have to be sure it fits your body. First, measure your **draw length**. Draw length is how far you draw back the arrow from the bow. Next, measure your **draw weight**. Find a bow that you can pull back without straining too hard. Draw weight increases by 10-pound (4.5-kilogram) increments. To hunt with accuracy, you need to be able to have a draw weight of at least 40 pounds (18 kg).

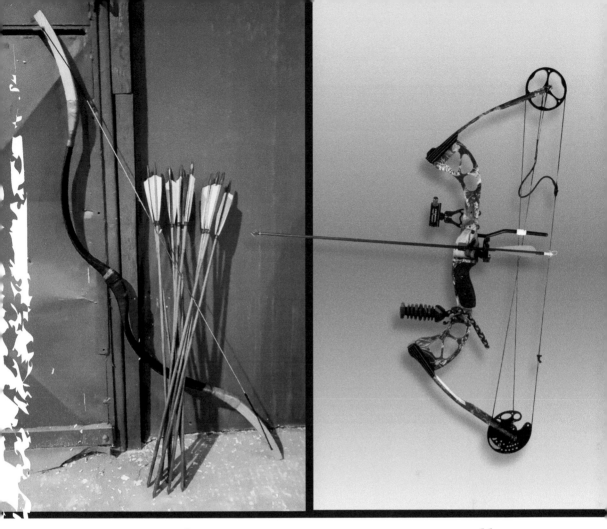

recurve bow   **compound bow**

A quiver of arrows

You'll need arrows to bowhunt, of course! Arrows have different kinds of tips. Field point tips are narrow and used when practicing on targets. Hunters use broadhead tips. These arrows are wide, flat, and sharp.

Other gear includes a **quiver**, which holds the arrows. Armguards help protect your bow arm. A release helps you let go of the bowstring.

Sights are another important piece of gear. They help you aim. One sight is a bow sight. It is a larger circle that fits on your bow. The other sight is a peep sight. It's a much smaller circle that makes a hole in the string. You must look through both sights to aim with accuracy.

Arrow Evolution

All arrows used to be made from wood and real feathers. They can still be made that way today. However, most arrows are now made from aluminum, carbon, or plastic with carbon. These are very strong but light materials.

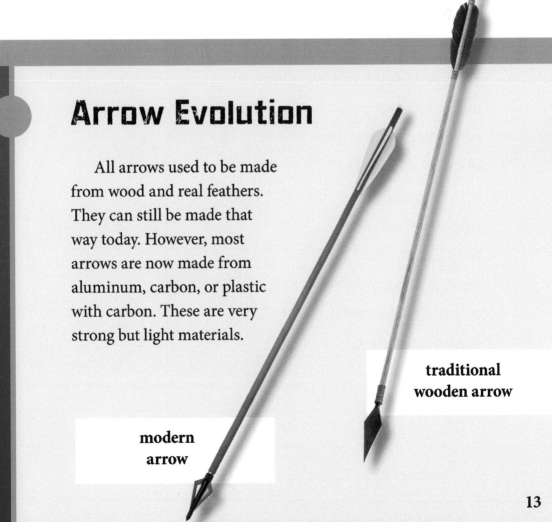

traditional wooden arrow

modern arrow

13

Chapter 3

SAFELY SHOOTING A BOW AND ARROW

Shooting a bow and arrow safely can be taught in a series of steps. When you stand, your feet should be shoulder-width apart. Your body should be 90 degrees to the target. The arm that grips the bow should point at the target. Keep your gripping hand loose. Use the web of your hand, or the skin between your thumb and pointer finger, to hold the bow just steady enough to aim. If you hold it too tight, the bow will twist.

A person aims a recurve bow.

A person aims a compound bow.

When you draw the arrow back, push your grip hand, or bow arm, toward the target. Do not completely straighten, or lock, your elbow. Pull the string back with your other hand, or release hand. Use all your strength to pull it across your chest.

When you draw back the bow, stop pulling at your anchor point. This can be any spot that feels most comfortable to you. Maybe it's your jaw or your ear. Just pick the same spot on your face every time. You'll let go of the arrow from that spot. Using the same anchor point every time helps your shot be more accurate.

A hunter pulls the arrow to his anchor point.

An archer aims by looking through the sights.

Use your sights to aim. When you look through them, keep both eyes open. Zero in on the exact spot you want to hit.

On a compound bow, release the arrow by pulling the trigger. On a recurve bow, let it go. Stay still for one second. Lower the bow after it hits the target.

A person aims a crossbow.

Bowhunting tips help you to stay safe as you learn the sport. Always make sure a responsible adult is with you. You may have to wear blaze orange or put it on your gear. Check your state's rules. This bright color helps other hunters see you and keeps you safe. Animals don't see it.

When it comes to shooting, never do it without an arrow **nocked** in the string. You need to get your **stance**, grip, and draw ready.

You might experience target panic. It can be nerve-racking to shoot an animal, especially if you are a new hunter. Target panic can include shooting before aiming, not drawing the arrow enough, or not holding the bow steady. To prevent target panic, hunters can try different things. They can buy release aids, aim without shooting, or use thinking exercises.

Chapter 4

RULES OF CONDUCT

When bowhunting, accuracy is a must. It's very important that the animal doesn't suffer. You don't just want to hit the animal. You want to kill it in seconds. Confidence is key, and that only comes with practice. You need to be confident you'll hit where you aim the arrow. Bowhunting courses can help you become a more confident hunter.

Before you hunt, make sure you can hit a plate from 30 yards (27 meters) away. Practice makes perfect. Try to hit it four out of five times. Hitting the plate five out of five times is what you're aiming for. When you're out hunting, wait until the animal is at the same distance from where you practiced.

A young archer practices shooting a bow and arrow.

FACT

Bowhunting courses are offered in all 50 states of the United States and required in many of them. Bowhunting education is also offered in more than 25 countries around the world.

An eight-point whitetail buck runs through a field.

So you've practiced enough to reach 80 to 100 percent accuracy and you think you're ready for the hunt. Not so fast! First, you must study the animal's **anatomy**. You need to know where an animal's lungs and heart are. Those are the organs you need to hit to kill an animal quickly. You can hit them by aiming at an animal's broadside, which is the side of an animal's body.

For example, a deer's heart and lungs are in its chest above its front legs. Aim the arrow at the deer's side. Do not angle the arrow too high or too low. Aim slightly higher and farther back than right behind the shoulder. A clean shot aimed in the correct place will kill the animal in seconds.

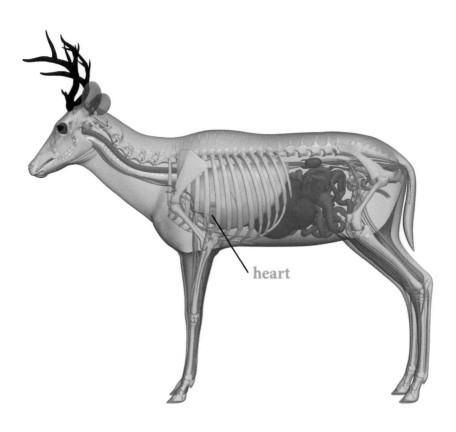

heart

The deer's heart is located beneath its lungs.

Follow signs, such as blood on the ground, to track an animal.

Once you shoot an animal, you need to find it. Wounded animals often take off running. If they're very quick, it can be difficult to see where you hit it.

An animal's behavior may give you clues about where it was hit. If you hit the heart or lungs, the animal should go down quickly. Even if it does run off, you may hear it fall in the woods.

If you don't see or hear where the animal fell, wait about 30 minutes to calm your nerves. With any luck, the animal will have died peacefully in that time. At that point, walk to where the animal was last standing. Look for the arrow or blood and start tracking. As you walk, look for signs of footprints, fur, and more blood.

FACT

Howard Hill has been voted into the Bowhunting Hall of Fame for being one of the best bowhunters of all time. In 1968, he was also one of the first hunters to use a bow in a movie.

Chapter 5

WHERE TO GO AND WHAT TO HUNT

Bowhunting is legal in all 50 of the United States and in many countries. Each location has its own rules, though. Some state rules describe which type of bow can be used. Some states limit the size of the bow. Other states limit the draw weight. Some rules say which arrows to use. States may also list which animals can be hunted. It is important to look up the rules of your area before you go hunting.

Hunters may decide to travel to a state because the animals they want to hunt are more plentiful there. Hunters may choose a state because there is more public land to hunt.

Bowhunting is also legal in some other countries around the world. Canada and New Zealand are two countries that welcome bowhunters.

In some places, such as New York State, it is legal to bowhunt for adult bears during certain times of the year.

FACT

The largest North American game to be killed with a bow is a black bear in New Jersey. It weighed 700 pounds (318 kilograms). It was shot on October 14, 2019.

**Moose, the largest of the deer family, can grow
antlers up to 6 feet (2 m) across.**

There are almost as many animals to bowhunt as
there are places to do it. Big game include whitetail deer,
mule deer, pronghorn, caribou, moose, and elk. Smaller
game include coyotes and turkeys. Even smaller game,
such as squirrels and rabbits, can be bowhunted. But
that's not all! You can try hunting alligators and even
fish. Bowhunting for fish is called bowfishing.

Bowhunting is a great sport for any hunter who enjoys a challenge. It takes practice, skill, and responsibility. Once you've mastered archery, you can challenge yourself with an exciting hunt!

A hunter aims his bow at something in the water.

GLOSSARY

anatomy (uh-NA-tuh-mee)—the scientific study of the body and how its parts are arranged

archery (AR-chuh-ree)—the sport of shooting at targets using a bow and arrow

camouflage (KA-muh-flahzh)—coloring or covering that makes animals, people, and objects look like their surroundings

draw (DRAW)—to pull something

draw length (DRAW LENGTH)—how far back one draws the arrow from the bow

draw weight (DRAW WATE)—a measurement of how much strength it takes to pull a bowstring back

nock (NOK)—to fit an arrow against a bowstring

precise (pri-SISSE)—very accurate or exact

quiver (KWIV-ur)—a container for arrows

sight (SITE)—a device on a bow that helps aim an arrow

stance (STANS)—the position of one's feet and body

READ MORE

Downs, Kieran. *Archery.* Minnetonka, MN: Bellwether Media, 2020.

Omoth, Tyler. *Bowhunting.* Lake Elmo, MN: Focus Readers, 2018.

Simons, Lisa M. Bolt. *Go Whitetail Deer Hunting!* North Mankato, MN: Capstone Press, 2022.

INTERNET SITES

Driven with Pat & Nicole
drivenhunter.com

Hunting Grouse
video.nationalgeographic.com/tv/0000014a-efff-dcdf-afcf-ffff55520000

Lancaster Archery: "How to Shoot a Deer From a Deer Stand"
lancasterarchery.com/blog/video/how-to-shoot-deer-from-a-tree-stand/

INDEX